Woody Guthrie
FOR UKULELE

Cover Photograph by Al Aumuller. Courtesy of Woody Guthrie Publications, Inc.

ISBN 978-1-4803-7025-8

Ludlow Music, Inc.

TRO The Richmond Organization

EXCLUSIVELY DISTRIBUTED BY

HAL•LEONARD®
CORPORATION
7777 W. BLUEMOUND RD. P.O. BOX 13819 MILWAUKEE, WI 53213

Visit Hal Leonard Online at
www.halleonard.com

Deportee
(Plane Wreck at Los Gatos)

Words by Woody Guthrie
Music by Martin Hoffman

mi - gos, Je - sús y Ma - ri - a. _____ You won't have your

names when you ride the big air - plane; all they will

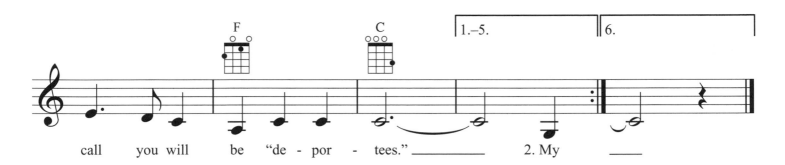

call you will be "de - por - tees." _____ 2. My _____

Additional Lyrics

2. My father's own father, he waded that river;
   They took all the money he made in his life.
   My brothers and sisters come working the fruit trees,
   And they rode the truck till they took down and died.

3. Some of us are illegal and some are not wanted;
   Our work contract's out and we have to move on.
   Six hundred miles to that Mexican border;
   They chase us like outlaws, like rustlers, like thieves.

4. We died in your hills and we died in your deserts.
   We died in your valleys and died on your plains.
   We died 'neath your trees and we died in your bushes.
   Both sides of the river, we died just the same.

5. The sky plane caught fire over Los Gatos Canyon,
   A fireball of lightning, and shook all our hills.
   Who are all these friends, all scattered like dry leaves?
   The radio says they are just deportees.

6. Is this the best way we can grow our big orchards?
   Is this the best way we can grow our good fruit?
   To fall like dry leaves to rot on my topsoil
   And be called by no name except "Deportees"?

Do Re Mi

Words and Music by Woody Guthrie

say, "You're num - ber four - teen thou - sand for to -

Chorus

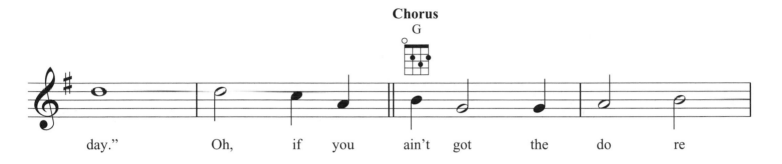

day." Oh, if you ain't got the do re

mi, folks, if you ain't got the do re

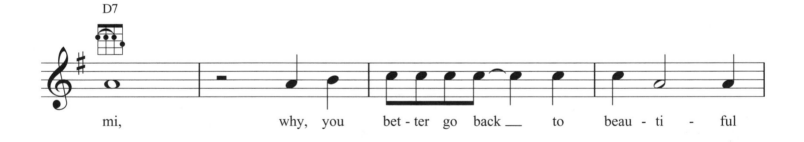

mi, why, you bet - ter go back ___ to beau - ti - ful

Tex - as, O - kla - ho - ma, Kan - sas, Geor - gia, Ten - nes -

see. ___ Cal - i - for - nia is a gar - den of

E - den,   a   par - a - dise   to   live   in   or

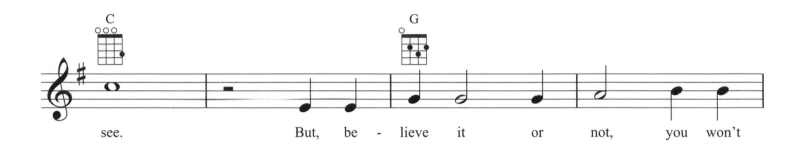

see.   But,   be - lieve   it   or   not,   you   won't

find   it   so   hot   if   you   ain't   got   the   do   re

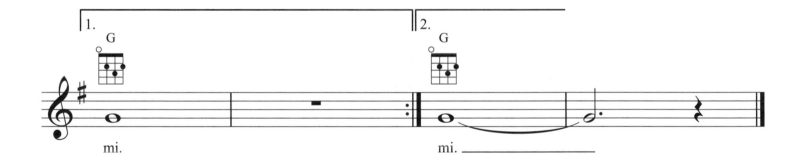

mi.   mi. _____

Additional Lyrics

2. If you want to buy you a home or farm,
That can't do nobody harm,
Or take your vacation by the mountains or sea,
Don't swap your old cow for a car;
You'd better stay right where you are.
You'd better take this little tip from me.
'Cause I look through the want ads every day,
But the headlines on the papers always say:

Greenback Dollar

Words and Music by Woody Guthrie

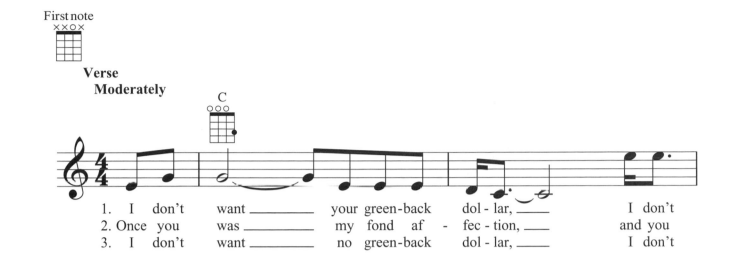

1. I don't want _____ your green-back dol - lar, _____ I don't
2. Once you was _____ my fond af - fec - tion, _____ and you
3. I don't want _____ no green-back dol - lar, _____ I don't

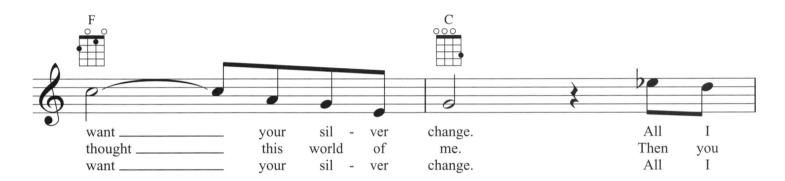

want _____ your sil - ver change. All I
thought _____ this world of me. Then you
want _____ your sil - ver change. All I

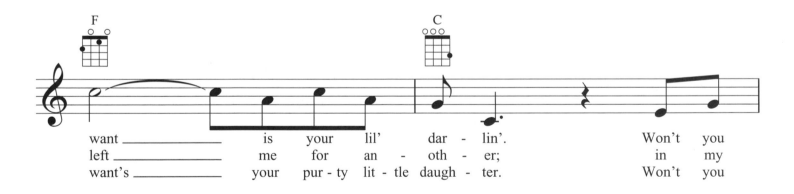

want _____ is your lil' dar - lin'. Won't you
left _____ me for an - oth - er; in my
want's _____ your pur - ty lit - tle daugh - ter. Won't you

take _____ me back a - gain?
grave _____ I'd rath - er be.
take _____ me back a - gain?

Going Down the Road

(I Ain't Going to Be Treated This Way)

Words and Music by Woody Guthrie and Lee Hays

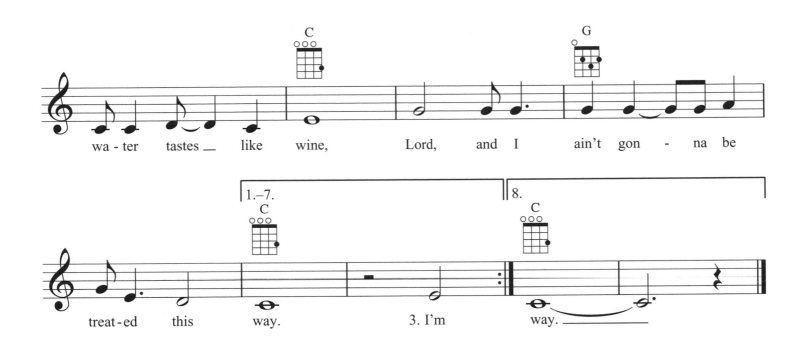

wa-ter tastes __ like wine,   Lord,   and I   ain't gon - na be

treat-ed this way.   3. I'm   way. _____

Additional Lyrics

3. I'm goin' where them dust storms never blow.
   I'm goin' where them dust storms never blow.
   I'm goin' where them dust storms never blow, blow, blow,
   And I ain't gonna be treated this way.

4. They say I'm a dust bowl refugee.
   Yes, they say I'm a dust bowl refugee.
   They say I'm a dust bowl refugee, Lord, Lord,
   But I ain't gonna be treated this way.

5. I'm lookin' for a job at honest pay.
   I'm lookin' for a job at honest pay.
   I'm lookin' for a job at honest pay, Lord, Lord,
   And I ain't gonna be treated this way.

6. My children need three square meals a day.
   Now, my children need three square meals a day.
   My children need three square meals a day, Lord,
   And I ain't gonna be treated this way.

7. It takes a ten-dollar shoe to fit my feet.
   It takes a ten-dollar shoe to fit my feet.
   It takes a ten-dollar shoe to fit my feet, Lord, Lord,
   And I ain't gonna be treated this way.

8. Your two-dollar shoe hurts my feet.
   Your two-dollar shoe hurts my feet.
   Yes, your two-dollar shoe hurts my feet, Lord, Lord,
   And I ain't gonna be treated this way.

9. I'm blowin' down this old dusty road.
   I'm blowin' down this old dusty road.
   I'm blowin' down this old dusty road, Lord, Lord,
   And I ain't gonna be treated this way.

Hanuka Dance

Words and Music by Woody Guthrie

Mail Myself to You

Words and Music by Woody Guthrie

First note

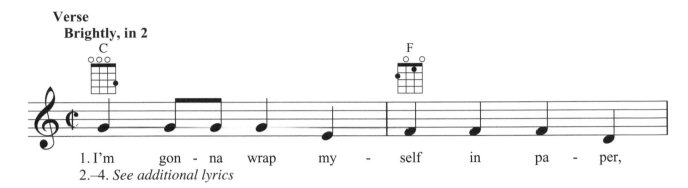

1. I'm gon-na wrap my-self in pa-per,
2.–4. *See additional lyrics*

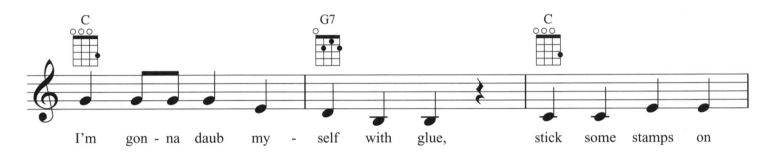

I'm gon-na daub my-self with glue, stick some stamps on

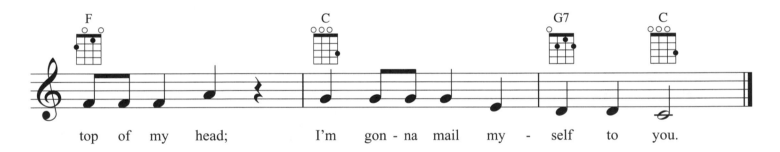

top of my head; I'm gon-na mail my-self to you.

Additional Lyrics

2. I'm gonna tie me up in a red string,
   I'm gonna tie blue ribbons, too.
   I'm gonna climb up in my mailbox,
   I'm gonna mail myself to you.

3. When you see me in your mailbox,
   Cut the string and let me out.
   Wash the glue off my fingers,
   Stick some bubblegum in my mouth.

4. Take me out of my wrapping paper,
   Wash the stamps off my head.
   Pour me full of ice cream sodies,
   Put me in my nice, warm bed.

Hesitating Beauty

Derivative Work of HESITATIN' BEAUTY

Words by Woody Guthrie
Music by Jeff Tweedy

First note

For your spar - kling, cock - y smile _____ I have
(2.) build a house and home _____ where the
(3.) ram - ble hand in hand a - cross the

walked a mil - lion miles, beg - ging you to come and wed me in the
flow - ers come to bloom. A - round our yard I'll nail a fence so
grass - es of our land. I'll kiss you for each leaf on ev - 'ry

spring. Why do you, my ___ dear, de - lay? What makes you
high that the boys with peep - ing eyes can - not
tree. We can bring our kids to play where the

laugh and turn a - way? You're a hes - i - tat - ing beau - ty, Nor - a
see that an - gel face of my hes - i - tat - ing beau - ty, Nor - a
dry leaves blow to - day if you'll quit your hes - i - tat - ing, Nor - a

Chorus

Lee.
Lee.
Lee.

Well, I know that you are itch-ing ___ to get mar-ried, ___ Nor-a Lee. And I

know I, oh, I am twitch-ing ___ for the same thing, Nor - a

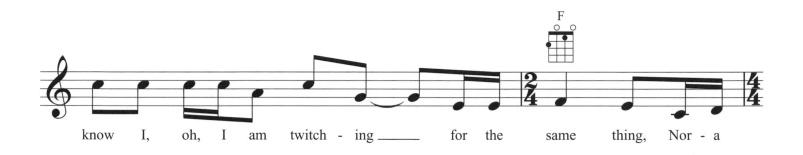

Lee. By the stars and clouds a - bove, we can spend our lives in love. (1.) You're a
(2., 3.) You ___

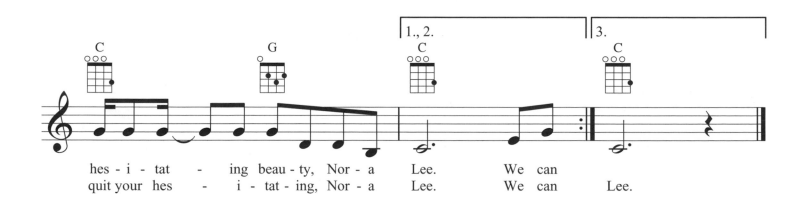

hes - i - tat - ing beau-ty, Nor - a Lee. We can
quit your hes - i - tat - ing, Nor - a Lee. We can Lee.

1., 2.

3.

Howdi Do

Words and Music by Woody Guthrie

First note

Verse
Bright Country feel, in 2

1. I stick out my lit-tle hand to ev-'ry wom-an, kid and
2.–6. *See additional lyrics*

man, and I shake it up and down, how-ji-do, how-ji-

do. Yes, I shake it up and down,_ how-ji-do. _____ How-dy

Chorus

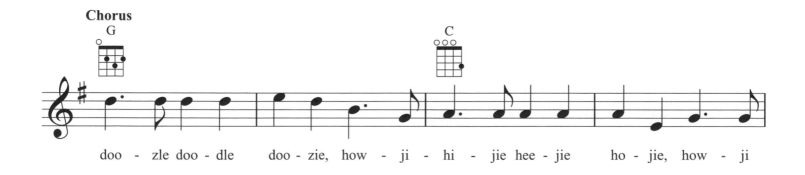

doo-zle doo-dle doo-zie, how-ji-hi-jie hee-jie ho-jie, how-ji

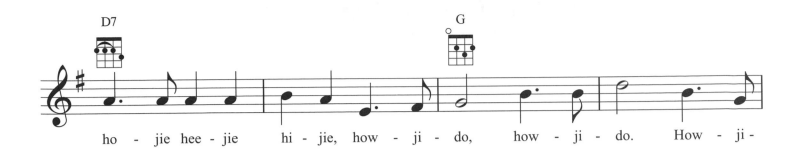

ho - jie hee - jie hi - jie, how - ji - do, how - ji - do. How - ji-

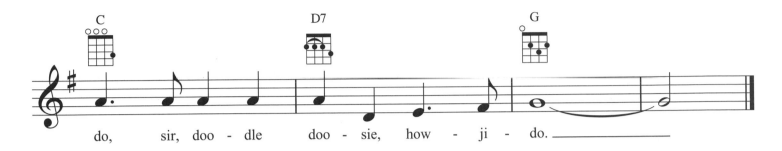

do, sir, doo - dle doo - sie, how - ji - do. _____

Additional Lyrics

2. And when you walk in my door,
   I will run across my floor,
   And I'll shake you by the hand,
   Howjido, howjido.
   Yes, I'll shake it up and down, howjido.

3. On my sidewalk, on my street,
   Any place that we do meet,
   Then I'll shake you by your hand,
   Howjido, howjido.
   Yes, I'll shake it up and down, howjido.

4. When I first jump out of bed,
   Out my window goes my head,
   And I shake it up and down,
   Howjido, howjido.
   I shake at all my windows, howjido.

5. I feel glad when you feel good,
   You brighten up my neighborhood,
   Shakin' hands with ev'rybody,
   Howjido, howjido.
   Shakin' hands with ev'rybody, howjido.

6. When I meet a dog or cat,
   I will rubby rub his back,
   Shakey, shakey, shakey paw,
   Howjido, howjido.
   Shaking hands with ev'rybody, howdy do.

I Ain't Got No Home

Words and Music by Woody Guthrie

First note

Verse
Moderately, in 2

1. I ain't got no home, I'm

2.–5. *See additional lyrics*

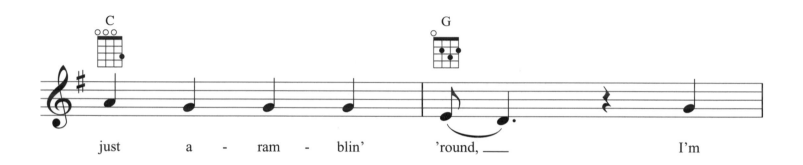

just a - ram - blin' 'round, ____ I'm

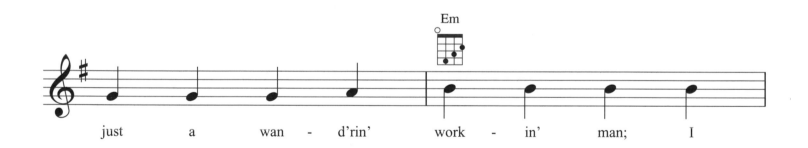

just a wan - d'rin' work - in' man; I

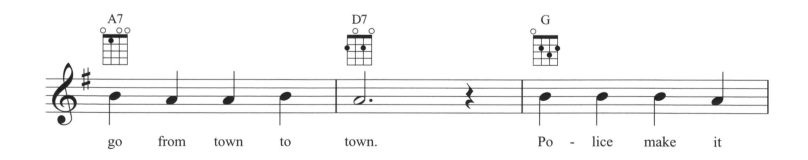

go from town to town. Po - lice make it

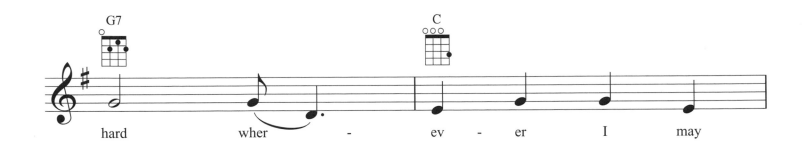

hard   wher - ev - er   I   may

go,   and   I   ain't   got   no

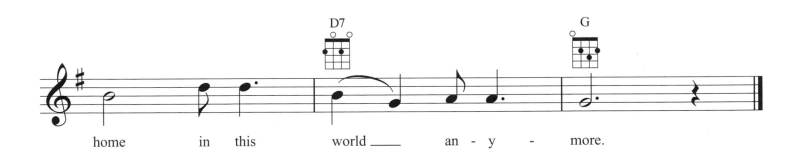

home   in   this   world ____ an - y - more.

Additional Lyrics

2. My brothers and my sisters are stranded on this road;
   It's a hot and dusty road that a million feet have trod.
   Rich man took my home and he drove me from my door,
   And I ain't got no home in this world anymore.

3. I was farmin' on the shares and always I was poor;
   My crops I lay into the banker's store.
   My wife took down and died upon my cabin floor,
   And I ain't got no home in this world anymore.

4. I mined in your mines and I gathered in your corn;
   I been working, mister, since the day that I was born.
   Now I worry all the time like I never did before,
   'Cause I ain't got no home in this world anymore.

5. Now as I look around, it's mighty plain to see.
   This wide and wicked world is a funny place to be.
   The gamblin' man is rich and the workin' man is poor,
   And I ain't got no home in this world anymore.

Little Seed

Words and Music by Woody Guthrie

Chorus

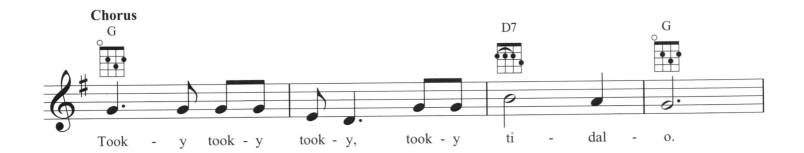

Took - y took - y took - y, took - y ti - dal - o.

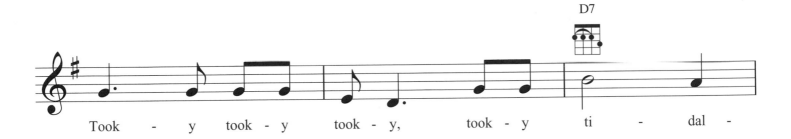

Took - y took - y took - y, took - y ti - dal -

o.   Let's all dance a - round ____ and see my

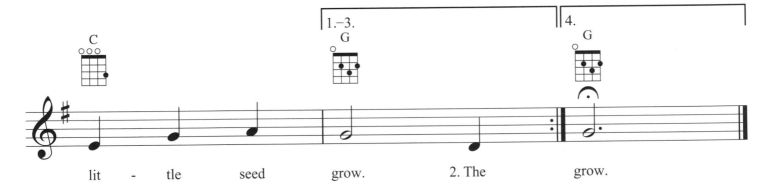

lit - tle seed grow.   2. The   grow.

Additional Lyrics

2. The rain, it come and it washed my ground.
   I thought my little seed was going to drown.
   I waded and I splashed and I carried my seed.
   I planted it again on some higher ground.

3. The sun got hot and my ground got dry.
   I thought my little seed would burn and die.
   I carried some water from a watering mill.
   I said, "Little seed, you can drink your fill."

4. The snow, it blowed; and the wind, it blew.
   My little seed grew and it grew and it grew.
   It grew up a cradle, all soft inside,
   And a baby was sleeping there, covered over with vines.

Pretty Boy Floyd

Words and Music by Woody Guthrie

First note

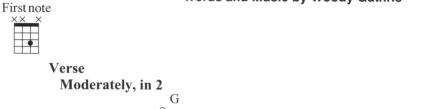

1. If you'll gath-er 'round me, chil-dren, a sto-ry I will tell 'bout
2.–12. *See additional lyrics*

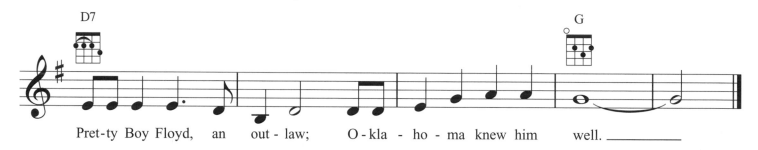

Pret-ty Boy Floyd, an out-law; O-kla-ho-ma knew him well. _____

Additional Lyrics

2. It was in the town of Shawnee,
   A Saturday afternoon,
   His wife beside him in the wagon
   As into town they rode.

3. There a deputy sheriff approached him
   In a manner rather rude,
   Using vulgar words of anger,
   And his wife, she overheard.

4. Pretty Boy grabbed a log chain
   And the deputy grabbed his gun.
   In the fight that followed,
   He laid that deputy down.

5. Then he took to the trees and timber,
   Along the river shore,
   Hiding on the river bottom,
   And he never come back no more.

6. Yes, he took to the trees and timber
   To live a life of shame.
   Every crime in Oklahoma
   Was added to his name.

7. But many a starvin' farmer
   The same old story told,
   How the outlaw paid their mortgage
   And saved their little home.

8. Others tell you 'bout a stranger
   That comes to beg a meal.
   Underneath his napkin,
   Left a thousand-dollar bill.

9. It was in Oklahoma City,
   It was on a Christmas day,
   There was a whole car load of groceries;
   Come with a note to say:

10. "Well, you say that I'm an outlaw,
    You say that I'm a thief.
    Here's a Christmas dinner
    For the families on relief."

11. Yes, as through this world I've wandered,
    I've seen lots of funny men.
    Some will rob you with a six-gun,
    And some with a fountain pen.

12. And as through your life you travel,
    Yes, as through your life you roam,
    You won't never see an outlaw
    Drive a family from their home.

So Long It's Been Good to Know Yuh
(Dusty Old Dust)

Words and Music by Woody Guthrie

First note
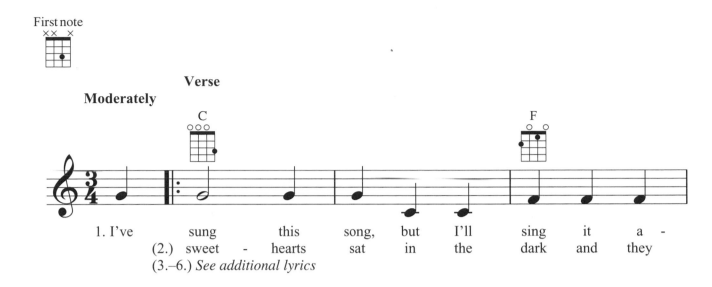

Verse

Moderately

1. I've sung this song, but I'll sing it a-
(2.) sweet - hearts sat in the dark and they
(3.–6.) *See additional lyrics*

gain of the peo - ple I've met and the
sparked. They _____ hugged and they kissed in that

plac - es I've been, of some of the
dust - y old dark. They sighed and they

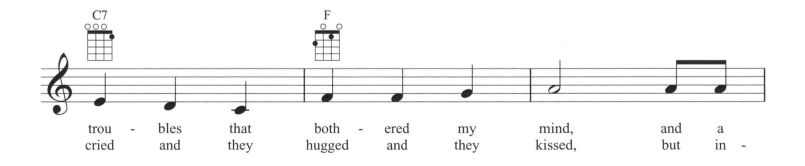

trou - bles that both - ered my mind, and a
cried and that they hugged and they kissed, but in -

lot   of   good   peo - ple   that   I've   left   be -
stead _____ of   mar - riage,   that   they   talked _____ like

Chorus

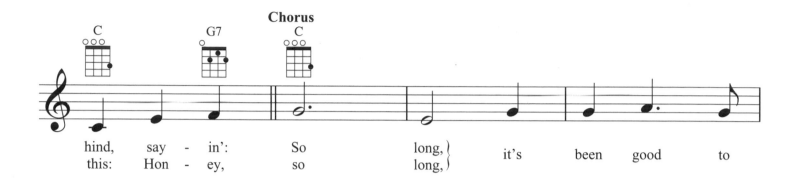

hind,   say - in':   So   long,}   it's   been   good   to
this: Hon - ey,   so   long,}   it's   been   good   to

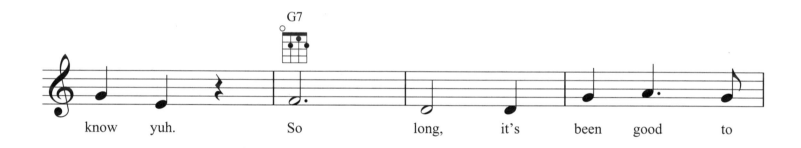

know   yuh.   So   long,   it's   been   good   to

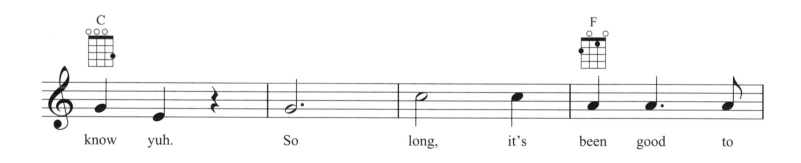

know   yuh.   So   long,   it's   been   good   to

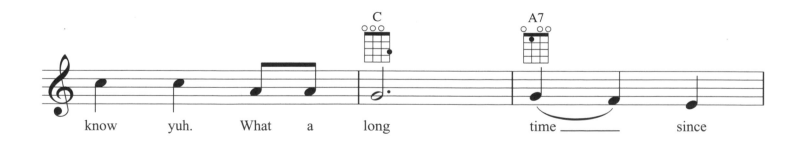

know   yuh.   What   a   long   time _____ since

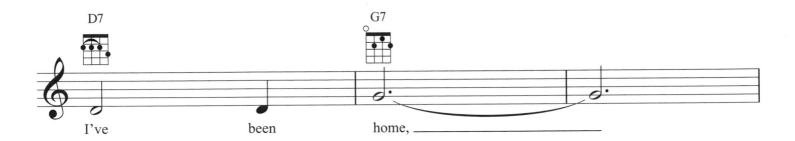

I've been home, _____

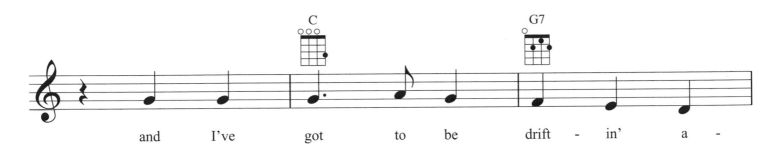

and I've got to be drift - in' a -

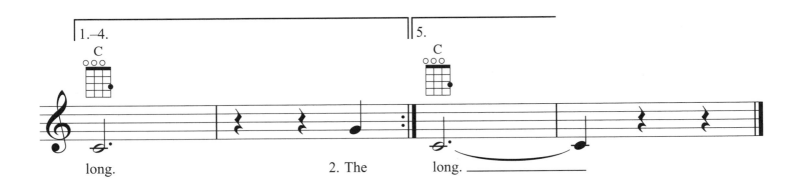

long.   2. The   long. _____

Additional Lyrics

3. I went to your family and asked them for you.
   They all said, "Take her, oh, take her, please do!
   She can't cook or sew and she won't scrub your floor."
   So I put on my hat and tiptoed out the door, saying:

4. I walked down the street to the grocery store.
   It was crowded with people, both rich and both poor.
   I asked the man how his butter was sold;
   He said, "One pound of butter for two pounds of gold." I said:

5. My telephone rang and it jumped off the wall.
   That was the preacher a-making a call.
   He said, "We're waitin' to tie the knot;
   You're gettin' married, believe it or not!"
   (Skip Chorus)

6. The church it was jammed, the church it was packed;
   The pews were so crowded from front to the back.
   A thousand friends waited to kiss my new bride,
   But I was so anxious I rushed her outside. Told them:

Ramblin' 'Round

Words by Woody Guthrie
Music based on "Goodnight, Irene" by Huddie Ledbetter and John Lomax

First note

Verse
Moderately

1. Ram - blin' a - round your cit - y, _____
(2.–6.) *See additional lyrics*

ram - blin' a - round your

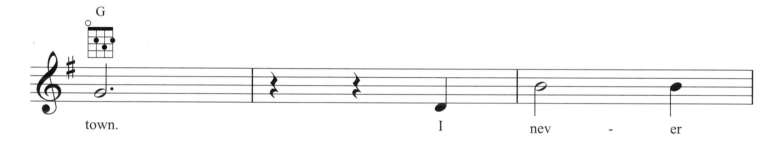

town. I nev - er

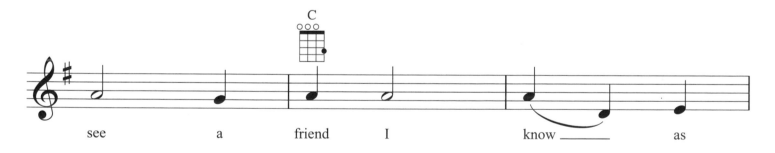

see a friend I know _____ as

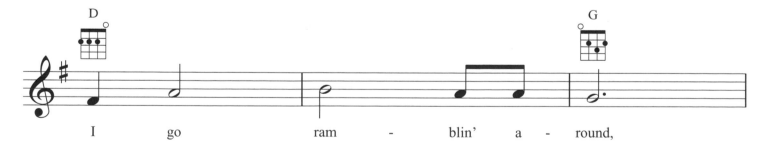

I go ram - blin' a - round,

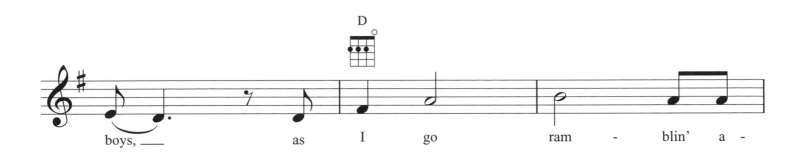

boys, _____ as I go ram - blin' a -

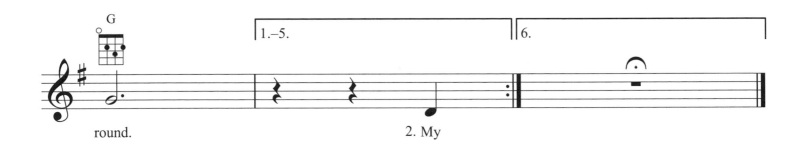

round. 2. My

Additional Lyrics

2. My sweetheart and my parents
   I left in my old home town.
   I'm out to do the best I can
   As I go ramblin' around, boys,
   As I go ramblin' around.

3. The peach trees, they are loaded,
   The limbs are bendin' down.
   I pick 'em all day for a dollar, boys,
   As I go ramblin' around,
   As I go ramblin' around.

4. Sometimes the fruit gets rotten,
   Falls down on the ground.
   There's a hungry mouth for ev'ry peach
   As I go ramblin' around, boys,
   As I go ramblin' around.

5. I wish that I could marry,
   I wish I could settle down.
   But I can't save a penny, boys,
   As I go ramblin' 'round,
   As I go ramblin' 'round.

6. My mother prayed that I would be
   A man of some renown.
   But I am just a refugee, boys,
   As I go ramblin' 'round,
   As I go ramblin' 'round.

Riding in My Car

Words and Music by Woody Guthrie

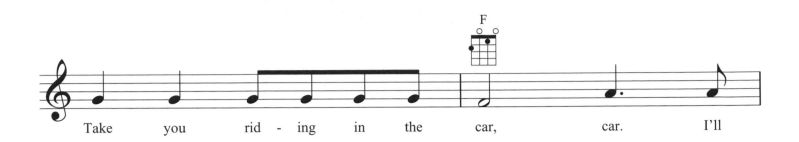

Take you rid - ing in the car, car. I'll

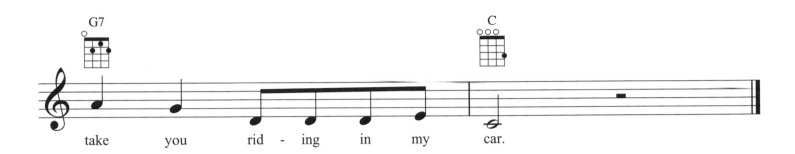

take you rid - ing in my car.

Additional Lyrics

2. Click, clack, open up the door, girls.
   Click, clack, open up the door, boys.
   Front door, back door, clickety clack,
   I'll take you riding in my car.

3. Climb, climb, rattle on the front seat.
   Spree I spraddle on the back seat.
   I turn my key, I step on the starter,
   I'll take you riding in my car.

4. Engine, it goes brrrm, brrrm.
   Engine, it goes brrrm, brrrm.
   Front seat, back seat, boys and girls,
   Take you riding in my car.

5. Trees and houses walk along.
   Trees and houses walk along.
   A truck and a car and a garbage can,
   Take you riding in my car.

6. Ships and little boats chug along.
   Ships and little boats chug along.
   Chug chugga chug, chuggy chug chug,
   Take you riding in my car.

7. I'm gonna let you blow the horn.
   I'm gonna let you blow the horn.
   Honk honk honk and beep beep beep,
   Take you riding in my car.

8. I'm gonna take you home again;
   I'm gonna zoom you home again;
   Brmmm brummm brummmm, we're rolling home,
   I'll take you home in my car.

The Sun Jumped Up

Words by Woody Guthrie
Music by Tim O'Brien

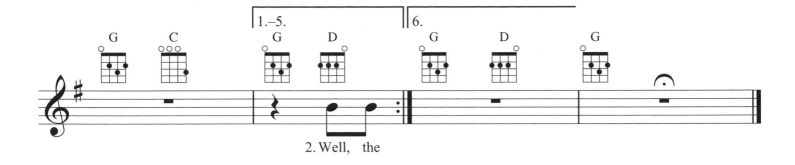

2. Well, the

Additional Lyrics

2. Well, the woman got the kid all fed
   By six fifteen this morning,
   And I had done made up our bed
   By six fifteen this morning.
   Well, the baby played on dancing feet
   And the woman stirred up a bite to eat,
   But that dream still pounded in my head
   At six fifteen this morning.

3. Well, I walked to work and the sun got warm
   At seven fifteen this morning.
   I held my lunch pail under my arm
   At seven fifteen this morning.
   Well, that dream kept ringing in my ear
   And getting plainer and coming clearer,
   Getting bigger and drawing near
   At seven fifteen this morning.

4. Well, I guess you know how some dreams are
   At eight fifteen this morning.
   You can't remember what they are
   At eight fifteen this morning.
   Well, I scratched my head at the factory gate
   And I run to keep from being late,
   And the clock said fifteen after eight
   At eight fifteen this morning.

5. Well, I waved to the boss and I talked to my friends
   At nine fifteen this morning.
   I was fishing around inside my brain
   At nine fifteen this morning.
   Well, I seen my dream like a haze or a snatch
   Or a blaze from some old fiery match,
   But the rest of my dream I could not catch
   At nine fifteen this morning.

6. So, at fifteen minutes after ten
   Or ten fifteen this morning,
   I told my trouble to all my friends
   At ten fifteen this morning.
   Well, I told them my dream was as plain as day,
   And how it run like a rabbit away.
   They said, "Keep trying if it takes all day!"
   At ten fifteen this morning.

This Land Is Your Land

Words and Music by Woody Guthrie

Additional Lyrics

3. When the sun came shining, and I was strolling,
   And the wheat fields waving, and the dust clouds rolling,
   As the fog was lifting, a voice was chanting:
   This land was made for you and me.

4. As I went walking, I saw a sign there,
   And on the sign it said, "No Trespassing,"
   But on the other side it didn't say nothing;
   That side was made for you and me.

5. In the shadow of the steeple, I saw my people.
   By the relief office, I saw my people.
   As they stood there hungry, I stood there asking:
   Is this land made for you and me?

6. Nobody living can ever stop me
   As I go walking that freedom highway.
   Nobody living can ever make me turn back;
   This land was made for you and me.

This Morning I Am Born Again

Words by Woody Guthrie
Music by Slaid Cleaves

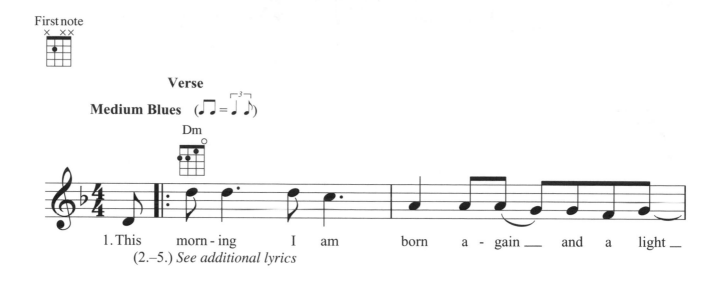

Verse
Medium Blues

1. This morn-ing I am born a-gain — and a light —
(2.–5.) *See additional lyrics*

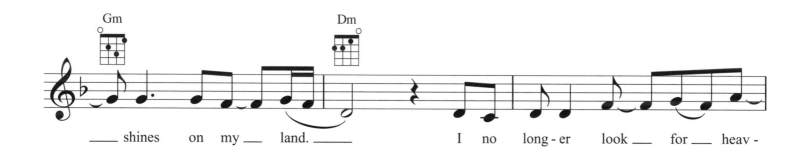

— shines on my — land. — I no long-er look — for — heav-

-en in your death-ly dis-tant land. — I do not want — your

pearl-y gates, — don't want — your streets of — gold. — This

morn - ing   I   am ___   born ___   a - gain ___   and   a   light _

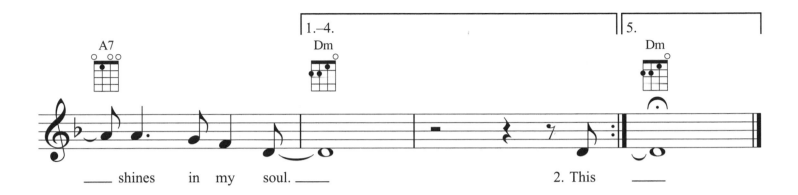

___ shines   in   my   soul. ___   2. This   ___

Additional Lyrics

2. This morning I am born again, I am born again complete.
   I stood up above my troubles and I stand on my two feet.
   My hand, it feels unlimited, my body feels like the sky.
   I feel at home in the universe and where yonder planets fly.

3. This morning I am born again; my past is dead and gone.
   This great eternal moment is my great eternal dawn.
   Each drop of blood within me, each breath of life I breathe,
   Is united with these mountains and the mountains with the seas.

4. I feel the sun upon me; its rays crawl through my skin.
   I breathe the life of Jesus and old John Henry in.
   I give myself, my heart, my soul, to give some friend a hand.
   This morning I am born again; I am in the promised land.

5. This morning I am born again and the light shines on the land.
   I no longer look for heaven in your deathly distant land.
   I do not want your pearly gates, don't want your streets of gold.
   And I do not want your mansion, for my heart is never cold.

This Train Is Bound for Glory

New Words and Music Adaptation by Woody Guthrie

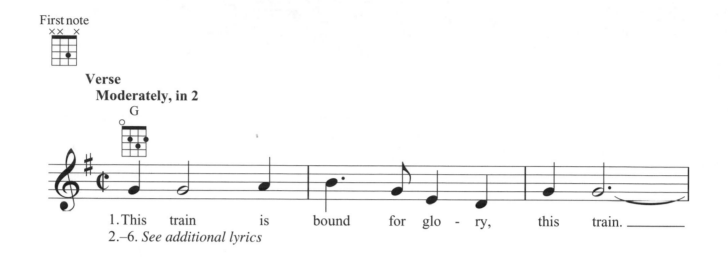

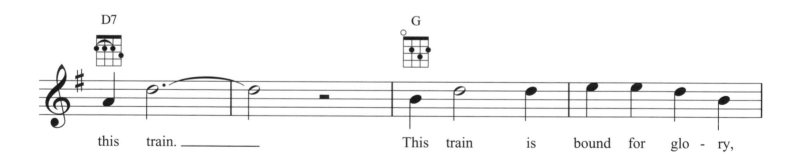

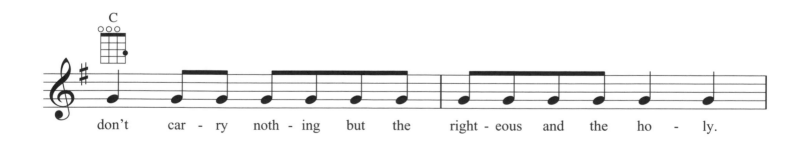

This train is bound for glo - ry, this train. _____

Additional Lyrics

2. This train don't carry no gamblers, this train.
   This train don't carry no gamblers, this train.
   This train don't carry no gamblers,
   Liars, thieves, nor big-shot ramblers.
   This train is bound for glory, this train.

3. This train don't carry no liars, this train.
   This train don't carry no liars, this train.
   This train don't carry no liars,
   She's streamlined and a midnight flyer.
   This train don't carry no liars, this train.

4. This train don't carry no smokers, this train.
   This train don't carry no smokers, this train.
   This train don't carry no smokers,
   Two-bit liars, small-time jokers.
   This train don't carry no smokers, this train.

5. This train don't carry no con men, this train.
   This train don't carry no con men, this train.
   This train don't carry no con men,
   No wheeler-dealers, here-and-gone men.
   This train don't carry no con men, this train.

6. This train don't carry no rustlers, this train.
   This train don't carry no rustlers, this train.
   This train don't carry no rustlers,
   Sidestreet walkers, two-bit hustlers.
   This train is bound for glory, this train.

Union Maid

Words and Music by Woody Guthrie
Melody based on a traditional theme

First note

Verse
With spirit, in 2

1. There once was a un - ion maid who nev - er was a -
2., 3. *See additional lyrics*

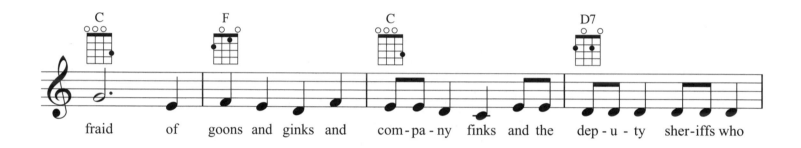

fraid of goons and ginks and com-pa-ny finks and the dep-u-ty sher-iffs who

made the raids. She went to the un - ion hall when a meet-ing it was

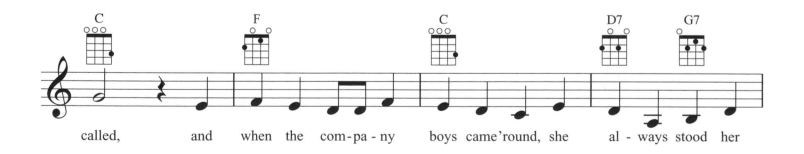

called, and when the com-pa-ny boys came 'round, she al - ways stood her

Chorus

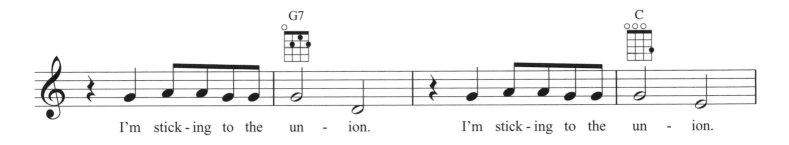

Additional Lyrics

2. This union maid was wise to the tricks of company spies.
   She never got fooled by a company stool; she'd always organize the guys.
   She always got her way when she struck for higher pay.
   She'd show her card to the company guard, and this is what she'd say:

3. You gals who want to be free, just take a little tip from me:
   Get you a man who's a union man and join the Ladies' Auxiliary.
   Married life ain't hard when you've got a union card.
   A union man has a happy life when he's got a union wife.

Way Over Yonder in the Minor Key

Words by Woody Guthrie
Music by Billy Bragg

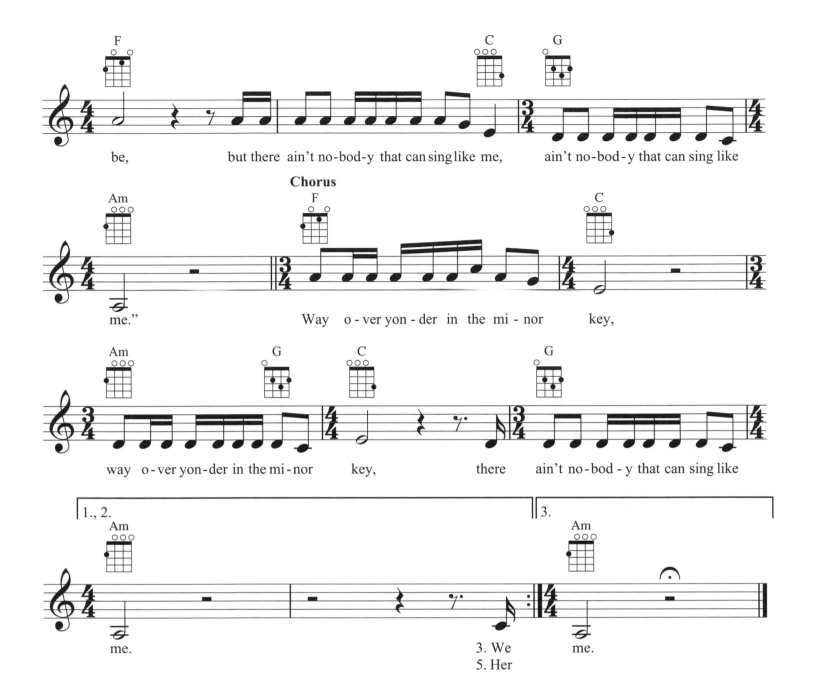

Additional Lyrics

3. We walked down by the Buckeye Creek
   To see the frog eat the goggle-eye bee,
   To hear that west wind whistle to the east.
   There ain't nobody that can sing like me,
   Ain't nobody that can sing like me.

4. Oh, my little girly, will you let me see
   Way over yonder where the wind blows free?
   Nobody can see in our holler tree
   And there ain't nobody that can sing like me,
   Ain't nobody that can sing like me.

5. Her mama cut a switch from a cherry tree
   And laid it on to she and me.
   It stung lots worse than a hive of bees,
   But there ain't nobody that can sing like me,
   Ain't nobody that can sing like me.

6. Now I have walked a long, long ways,
   And I still look back to my tanglewood days.
   I've led lots of girls since then to stray,
   Saying, "Ain't nobody that can sing like me,
   Ain't nobody that can sing like me."